THE CHANGING FACE OF
ITALY

Text by KATHRYN BRITTON
Photographs by CHRIS FAIRCLOUGH

RAINTREE
STECK-VAUGHN
PUBLISHERS

A Harcourt Company

Austin   New York
www.raintreesteckvaughn.com

Library of Congress Cataloging-in-Publication Data is available upon request

ISBN 0-7398-5490-9

Printed in Italy. Bound in the United States.

1 2 3 4 5 6 7 8 9 0 LB 06 05 04 03 02

Acknowledgments

The publishers would like to thank the following for their contributions to this book: Rob Bowden – statistical research; Nick Hawken – illustrations on pages 7, 20, 26, 36 and 42; Peter Bull – map on page 5. All photographs are by Chris Fairclough except: Camera Press 42; Jodi Hilton 24, 31; Popperfoto 10, 40.

Contents

1 Milan: City of Glamour.........................4

2 Past Times 6

3 Landscape and Climate........................8

4 Natural Resources 14

5 The Changing Environment...............20

6 The Changing Population...................26

7 Changes at Home 30

8 Changes at Work 40

9 The Way Ahead 44

Glossary 46

Further Information 47

Index 48

1 Milan: City of Glamour

Situated in the north of Italy, near Switzerland and close to the other major Italian cities of Turin and Genoa, Milan is ideally situated to be a business and financial center. Many roads and railways run from Milan toward France, Switzerland, and Austria, making it relatively cheap for local companies to transport goods to and from the rest of Europe.

As well as being a world-famous fashion center, Milan is also a media city. It is home to three major Italian television channels and some of the country's most widely read newspapers, including *Sole 24 Ore* (Italy's main financial newspaper), *Il Corriere della Sera* (a daily newspaper), and the current affairs magazines *Panorama* and *Espresso*.

In the past, the city's major industries included machinery, textiles, graphics, and chemical manufacturing. Today, however, service industries (such as tourism, transportation and information technology) are the main sources of employment.

As many as 1.5 million people live in Milan, and another 1.5 million come into the city to work every day. Not surprisingly, this causes huge traffic problems, especially as the roads in the center of town are very small and winding. Even though the city planners built large circular avenues around the downtown areas in the 1950s, there are still lots of traffic jams. Yet despite the excellent public transportation system, which includes buses, trains, and trams, many people still choose to drive into the city. After all, their cars are part of their glamorous lifestyle—and glamour is everything in Milan.

▲ *La Galleria shopping center in Milan. This beautiful mall has many shops and cafés—the perfect place for the glamorous Milanese to be seen!*

▶ *Milan's ultra-modern public transportation system encourages people to leave their cars at home.*

▲ This map shows the major geographical features of Italy, and other places mentioned in this book.

ITALY: KEY FACTS

Area: 116,347 square miles (301,338 sq km)

Population: Nearly 58 million

Population density: 476 people per square mile (191 per sq km)

Capital city: Rome (2.65 million)

Other main cities: Milan (1.3 million), Naples (1 million), Turin (0.9 million), Palermo (0.7 million), Genoa (0.6 million)

Highest mountain: Monte Bianco (Mont Blanc) 15,781 feet (4,810 m)

Longest river: The Po 405 miles (652 km)

Main language: Italian

Main religion: Roman Catholicism

Currency: Euro

Past Times

Over 2,000 years ago, Italy's capital city, Rome, became the most powerful city in the western world. Over the next thousand years, the strength of the Roman army was to see the Roman Empire expand to include most of western Europe, the Middle East, and northern Africa. Roman engineering, technology, and art were to have a lasting effect on the development of these regions.

Almost a thousand years after the fall of the Roman Empire, Italy was one of the least powerful countries in western Europe. Italians felt that they needed a strong and determined leader. In 1922, Benito Mussolini established an extreme right-wing fascist government. Italy entered World War II as a German ally in 1939. During the war, Mussolini's fascist government fell, and Italy declared war on Germany. The country was then defeated and occupied by the Germans.

In 1945, at the end of World War II, Italy's economy was in ruins and had to be rebuilt. The Americans offered the Italians financial aid, in the form of the European Recovery Fund (also known as the Marshall Plan). Then, in the 1950s, Italy joined the European Coal and Steel Community (ECSC) and the

▲ A Communist Party poster. The political upheavals of the 20th century have meant that both extreme right-wing and extreme left-wing political groups have support in Italy.

◄ Many Italians spend hours discussing politics—whatever their age. This local square in Pisa is the perfect place to meet and talk.

European Economic Community (EEC). Italy's membership of these two communities helped boost the economy, making it easier to import raw materials for manufacturing industries, to use workers from other European countries, and to trade with other ECSC and EEC members.

Today, the wealthy industrial regions of the north produce about three-quarters of the country's Gross National Product (GNP), whereas the south, with its largely rural population and lack of industry, contributes only about a quarter. This has caused deep divisions between the north and south of Italy. The Northern League Party, formed in 1977, gained strong electoral support in the early 1990s. It aims to free the economically powerful northern regions from Italy's central government in Rome. It has a strong following throughout the north.

Most Italians are very interested in politics and often go to meetings at political clubs. Demonstrations and protests are frequently organized, particularly by young people.

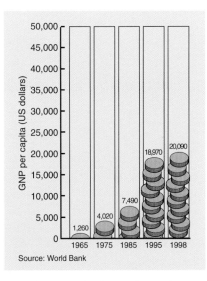

Source: World Bank

▲ *This graph shows how the GNP of Italy has increased over the past four decades.*

IN THEIR OWN WORDS

"My name is Vanessa. I'm 16 and I live in Ravenna. I worry that young Italians don't think enough about what is happening in the world. We need to act when we see injustice. Students in my school take action when things affect them. We organize sit-ins at school to protest about the education system—and even about the poor heating at school! Some students come just to get out of class, but luckily some of us take these demonstrations seriously. Sometimes we do manage to change things. But we also need to take action when things don't affect us directly. In this picture I'm reading a socialist newspaper, *Il Manifesto*. It encourages us to take an interest in national and international politics."

3 Landscape and Climate

Italy has a variety of landscapes: beautiful beaches, steep mountain ranges, and grassy plains. There are twenty national parks in Italy and more than 130 regional ones. These parks are home to much of Italy's wildlife.

Rivers and Lakes

The longest river in Italy is the Po. It begins in the north-west, just inside the French border, and flows for over 405 miles (652 km) across the north of the country from west to east, finally reaching the Adriatic Sea, south of Venice.

There are two other major rivers, the Tiber and the Adige. The Adige is 255 miles (410 km) long. Like the Po, it begins in the north of Italy, near the border with Austria, then flows down to the Adriatic Sea near Venice. The Tiber begins in the hills of Emilia-Romagna and flows for 252 miles (405 km), through Rome and out to sea at Ostia.

▲ *A river running through an alpine village.*

IN THEIR OWN WORDS

"My name is Alberto Re Bucci and I'm vice-president of the Regional Park of the Delta del Po. The park was established in 1988 and it is the largest regional park in Italy, covering a total of 185,328 acres (75,000 hectares). It has many different species of bird, including herons, ducks, and avocets. The park is important not only because it protects the wildlife, but also because it shows us that people and the government are beginning to care about the environment. Since the park was founded, there has been an increase in the number of birds and animals in the area."

The north of the country has three well-known lakes. The largest is Lake Garda (143 square miles [370 sq km]), followed by Maggiore (82 square miles [212 sq km]), and then Como (56 square miles [145 sq km]), the third largest but deepest lake at 1,345 feet (410 m). Although these lakes lie at the foot of the Alps, they have a relatively warm climate and are surrounded by groves of olive, orange, and lemon trees.

Mountains

Italy has three main mountain ranges. The Alps, in the northwest, extend from Italy to France and Switzerland. The Dolomites, to the northeast, lie between Italy and Austria. And the Apennines run down the center of the country, beginning in the northwest near Genoa and continuing down to the Straits of Messina (the "toe" of Italy). Monte Bianco is the highest mountain in Italy, and is often known by its French name of Mont Blanc. It stands at 15,781 feet (4,810 m) on the border with France.

▼ *Lake Garda in the Italian Alps. In the north of Italy people have the pleasure of living near both mountains and lakes.*

Volcanoes

Italy has two active volcanoes, Vesuvius and Etna. Vesuvius, which overlooks the city of Naples, is 4,196 feet (1,279 m) above sea level and last erupted in 1944. Etna is on the island of Sicily. At 10,902 feet (3,323 m) above sea level, it is the highest volcano in Europe. It also remains active. During an eruption in 2001, many businesses (restaurants and souvenir shops) that stood on the side of the volcano were completely destroyed. At night, rivers of lava can often be seen running down the mountainside, a constant reminder to local people of the dangers of living so close to a volcano.

Earthquakes

Volcanoes are not the only natural danger Italy faces.
Large areas of the country, especially the center and the south, are also at risk from earthquakes. Over the last century, there have been a number of serious earthquakes. The most severe was in Messina, Sicily, in 1908, when more than 60,000 people lost their lives.

▲ *Mount Etna in Sicily erupted for two weeks during July and August 2001.*

Coasts

Italy's coastline varies. In the east, along the Adriatic, are low-lying, sandy beaches, while the western Tyrrhenian coast is steeper and rockier. The islands off the coast of Italy, such as Sicily, Sardinia, and Capri, boast some spectacular beaches.

Unfortunately, human activity has caused a number of problems for the Italian coast. In many areas, piers or breakwaters have been built for tourists, and because of this construction the currents cannot move naturally. This has led to coastal erosion, which occurs when the sea level rises (often because of the changing climate) and the sea begins to "eat up" the beaches. The other problem is pollution. In the past, rivers that had been polluted by factory waste flowed into the sea. But new laws and regulations introduced by the EEC have greatly reduced sea pollution.

▲ *A public beach at Marina di Pisa in Tuscany. Many Italians prefer to pay to go to private beaches, which are often less crowded.*

IN THEIR OWN WORDS

"My name is Marco and I have a beach café on the Adriatic coast. August is our busiest month. Every year there are more tourists and they want more things to do—this year we have organized aerobics classes on the beach. We also organize evening events to keep all the vacationers happy. One of the biggest problems here is erosion—when the sea "eats up" the beach. On the bright side, the beach used to be polluted, but now things are getting better because new regulations mean that factories can't pollute the sea. We haven't had any pollution problems for a number of years—let's hope it stays that way."

Climate

The climate in the north of Italy is cooler than the climate in the south. The average temperature in January in the north is approximately 46 ° F (8° C), while in the south it is around 50 ° F (10° C). In July, the temperature in the north rises to around 72 ° F (22° C), while in the south it is normally 77–86 ° F (25–30° C). Occasionally, there are some particularly hot spells, when the temperature in both the north and the south soars to over 100° F (almost 40° C). There are also climatic differences between east and west. Wet currents come in from the Atlantic, while dry, cold ones come in from Eastern Europe.

▶ *Olive groves in central Italy. The varying climatic regions mean that all over the country different crops can be grown.*

IN THEIR OWN WORDS

"My name is Rodolfo and I'm a doctor in Milan. I come from the south of Italy but have lived in the north for the last fifteen years. Visitors to the north of Italy are often surprised by how cold and wet it can be here. They don't realize the variety of climates we have in Italy. I like the north but I miss the weather we have in Calabria, where I come from. Although the winters are cool in Calabria, it has quite a lot of sunshine for most of the year. In Milan, it is often foggy and damp in the winter and we can go for days without seeing the sun. As soon as the sun appears, my wife Angela and I come out into the mountains to do some walking. Fresh air and sunshine—what could be better!"

Different parts of Italy also get very different amounts of rain. For example, in Cagliari, on the island of Sardinia, there may be less than 9.8 inches (250 mm) of rain a year, while in Genoa on the Ligurian coast there may be almost 38.6 inches (980 mm).

Some scientists believe that recent high temperatures and floods show that the climate of Italy is changing. The regions of Liguria and Piemonte have suffered bad flooding since the 1990s, including seven major floods and many smaller, local ones.

▼ *The Grand Canal in Venice. Changes in the climate have caused serious flooding in this beautiful city.*

Floods in Venice

Venice, in particular, has been badly affected by the changing climate. The city is built on a group of eighteen islands in a lagoon called La Laguna Veneta. It suffered its worst-ever flood in 1966. St. Mark's Square was under 4.1 feet (1.25 m) of water for thirty-six hours and enormous damage was caused to the city's beautiful buildings. The only positive result was that people became more aware of the need to "Save Venice." In 1973, the government began investing in research on ways of reducing land settling and pollution. A lot of work has been done on designing mobile flood barriers but, because of political changes and the enormous amount of money involved, they still have not been built.

4

Natural Resources

Minerals

Italy's mineral resources are very scarce. There are some deposits of zinc, pyrites, and aluminum, but they are poor quality and scattered across the country. As it is too expensive to mine them, these minerals are imported instead. However, marble is mined for use in the building industry in Italy, and also for export.

Italy also has to import most of the iron and coal needed for its industries. Half of Italy's iron comes from Elba, an island off the west coast. In the past, there were coal deposits in Sardinia and Tuscany, but these mines closed down in the 1970s. Most of Italy's coal is now imported from the United States, other European countries, and even Japan.

▲ *The marble from this mine in Tuscany will be highly polished before it is used for building.*

IN THEIR OWN WORDS

"My name is Simona. I'm an engineer for the company AGIP, which extracts and produces natural gas and oil. The company I work for is one of the biggest in the world (in the top ten!). We have extracted almost all the gas that we can from Italian territory. We could extract more from the Adriatic Sea, but environmental groups are against it because they believe it would worsen the problem of coastal erosion. Because of this, many of my colleagues are sent abroad to work in places such as Nigeria and Kazakstan. Some of what we extract abroad is piped back to Italy, and what is left over is sold to other countries."

Energy Sources

Italy's most important natural resource is natural gas, which is found mainly in the valley around the Po River. In the 1950s it was also found in the south—in Basilicata, Sicily, and Puglia.

In the 1980s, Italy's industrial and domestic energy requirements started to grow more quickly. Its petroleum and gas deposits were no longer big enough to meet the demand, and more fuel had to be imported. Nowadays, Italy still imports more energy than it produces. In 2000, it imported almost 80 percent of its energy requirements.

One-fifth of the country's electricity is generated by water power. Seventeen out of Italy's twenty-one hydroelectric power stations are in the Alps. Italy did have a small number of nuclear power stations, but Italians were not happy about the use of nuclear energy. Following a referendum in 1988, Italy stopped using nuclear power.

Water Supply

Although Italy is a leading economic power in Europe, there are still some regions that do not have a regular water supply. Numerous towns in the south of the country, particularly in Sicily, have little or no water for months at a time. People are often forced to buy water from private sources, and, when building a home, they try to ensure that they have their own well.

▶ *In some areas of southern Italy, water is not always available. The people in this photo are collecting water from a public tap.*

Fishing

Despite Italy's extensive coastlines, the Italian fishing industry is not as successful as it might be. In 1997, for example, Italy imported as much fish as it produced (50.4 percent). However, there are some parts of the country that rely heavily on fishing as a source of employment. Mazara del Vallo, in Sicily, and San Benedetto del Tronto, in Marche, are two such towns. In these areas, fishing is not only a source of income but also a longstanding family tradition.

In recent years, coastline fishermen—those who fish under 11.8 miles (19 km) from the coast—have seen a decrease in the number of fish, due to pollution. Meanwhile, the boats that fish further out to sea have changed dramatically in the past few decades. They now have electronic systems to show the fishermen where the fish are, and machines for freezing and storing them. These storage systems are very important, as the fishermen can sometimes be at sea for days or weeks at a time.

▲ *A fishmonger's market stall. Italians travel for miles to buy good fish. This fish shop in Comacchio has customers from all over the northeast of the country.*

IN THEIR OWN WORDS

"My name is Roberto and I come from a family of fishermen. When I was a child I used to go out to sea with my father and my grandfather. It was wonderful, but very hard work.

"Now I make nets for the fishermen of my village, and my children work with me. It's a hard job and we hardly ever have a day off, but it's better than going out to sea every day. A lot of people from the north of Italy come here to spend their vacations fishing—and they come to eat our fish. It is fantastic!"

Fish Farming

The most significant change has been the increase in fish farming. Rather than waiting for the fish to reproduce when and where they please, they are now bred in lagoons or even out at sea, and harvested when needed. In 1985, fish farming produced 173,060 tons of fish, and by 1998 this had increased to 274,471 tons. While the traditional fishing industry has seen a fall in production, fish farming has been going from strength to strength.

▲ Fishing nets along the canals near Comacchio on the east coast of Italy. Inland fishing is very important to the Italian fishing industry.

Crops

Olives, grapes, rice, maize, tomatoes, and citrus fruits (such as oranges, tangerines, and lemons) are Italy's main crops. The north of the country, with its high rainfall, is very fertile. Farms here cultivate maize, wheat, and rice (which is exported in large quantities). However, it is almost impossible to grow anything in parts of the south and Sardinia because of their hot, dry climate and poor soil. Where cultivation can be carried out, the most common produce is citrus fruits, tomatoes, and olives. Unlike other crops, olives thrive in the dry conditions of the south, and the long, hot summers make their oil content higher. Italy is the biggest exporter of olive oil in the world.

In the wealthier north, more modern farming methods are used and the farmers have better machines and equipment. Because of the wetter climate, better soil, and more mechanization, yields in the north can be three times as high as in the south.

▲ *These men are conducting experiments in order to improve the quality of rice crops.*

Wine and Fruit

Most Italian regions produce and export wine. Fruit, too, is exported in large quantities—particularly apples, peaches, grapes, citrus fruit, and sugarbeet. Tomatoes and flowers are also widely cultivated. The country is gradually moving toward organic agriculture (which avoids the use of chemical weed-killers and insecticides). However, the pace of change is slow because it costs farmers more to grow organic crops, and consumers are not always willing to pay higher prices for their produce.

Livestock

Meat production in Italy is generally low, compared with other countries in southern Europe. And since the problems caused by cows being infected with BSE (bovine spongiform encephalopathy)—which is suspected of causing the fatal vCJD (variant Creutzfeldt-Jakob disease) in humans—sales of beef have fallen sharply. However, pig and poultry farming are currently expanding.

▲ In the arid regions of Italy, crops need to be irrigated for most of the year.

IN THEIR OWN WORDS

"My name is Luciano and I export fruit from Italy to England and Ireland. The peaches in this picture will be exported all over Europe. These days, we export a lot of organic fruit. This is the fastest-growing trend in Italy. There's a lot of cooperation between the producers, the distributors, and the sellers. With new technology, we now have systems that can guarantee certain qualities such as sweetness and ripeness, so that the supermarkets have exactly what they want when they want it. I export fruit from all over Italy. In the north, the producers work with more advanced technology, but in the south the farmers still use some old-fashioned methods."

5

The Changing Environment

From Country Life to City Life

In the mid-1950s, people began moving out from the countryside and into urban centers because of the new job opportunities available there. The rural population has been gradually declining ever since, while cities have increased in size every year. Now, almost 30 percent of the population of Italy is concentrated in about fifty municipalities, each with over 100,000 inhabitants. Thirteen of these municipalities have a population of over 250,000, ranging from Rome with 2,644,000 to Verona with 255,000.

Changes in Housing

The current trend for people to live in houses rather than apartments means that more and more land is being used for urban housing. Many city councils are doing their best to deal with the pollution caused by the increasing population and the growing numbers of cars and factories. Some have a policy whereby one tree is planted for every child that is born.

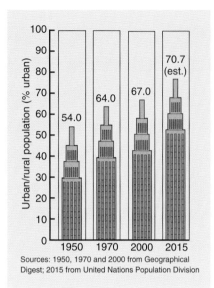

Sources: 1950, 1970 and 2000 from Geographical Digest; 2015 from United Nations Population Division

▲ *The percentage of Italians living in urban centers has continued to increase since 1950.*

▼ *Major cities such as Milan are now home to more Italians than ever before.*

In the past, construction in Italy has often been poorly planned and controlled. In some areas—particularly in the south—the natural landscape has been damaged by the building of hotels and housing. Much of Italy is subject to landslides, and many buildings were constructed on land that could be dangerous in the case of heavy rain. Since 1999, the government has clamped down on this. It may now even have to order the demolition of these dangerous buildings.

▲ *Construction being carried out in Casal Borsetti, on the Adriatic coast. Today, strict laws ensure that construction does minimal damage to Italy's natural environment.*

IN THEIR OWN WORDS

"My name is Claudia and I'm an engineer. I work on restoring old buildings and making them safe. We have so many beautiful buildings in Italy that are very, very old. Now many of them are in bad condition and need restoring—not only for their beauty, but also to make them safe for people. When they were built nobody thought about fire and safety regulations. Now we have many new regulations and laws that have been introduced to protect these buildings. It's very difficult to keep a building's original beauty and make sure it meets new safety regulations."

Air Pollution

Environmental pressure groups have worked hard at persuading the population and the government of the need to protect the environment. Now, levels of air pollution in Italian cities are constantly monitored. When the level of pollution is particularly high, the local authorities may close cities to traffic, even on a weekday. There are also a number of Sundays throughout the year (up to ten, depending on the region) when cities are closed to cars. On these occasions, people walk or use bicycles or public transportation.

▼ *Many Italian city councils rent out bikes. This encourages people to use transportation that does not create air pollution.*

IN THEIR OWN WORDS

"My name is Sabrina and I work for an organization that trains companies and their employees to be more environmentally friendly. We receive funding from the European Union, which is a big help. The small- and medium-sized companies don't really want to spend a lot of money in this field, even if they realize that it's important. However, some do want to give something back to their employees and the country— not just by producing goods, but also by protecting the environment. Now, many factories are even recycling their own trash. I think the media has a very important role in helping to inform and educate the population. We can see that, overall, public education is working."

Water Pollution

Factories in Italy are strictly monitored by local authorities to make sure that they are not letting their waste flow out into the rivers or seas. When the rivers of Italy become polluted, so too does the surrounding sea. In the past, this caused serious problems for the tourist industry, as swimmers stayed away from polluted water. Nowadays, partly due to government television advertising campaigns about the problems of pollution, Italians are beginning to behave more responsibly. Environmental groups often organize "cleaning days," when volunteers help clear trash from riverbanks and beaches.

▲ *Logging is one of the many industries that must be sure not to pollute rivers or beaches with its waste products.*

Electromagnetic Smog

Another form of pollution that is causing concern in Italy is electromagnetic smog, caused by the aerials and pylons needed for the latest telecommunications technology. There is some evidence that the radiation emitted by these devices can be dangerous to those living nearby. Fortunately, the government plans to enact laws ensuring that these pylons are placed at a safe distance from residential areas.

▲ *In the future, mobile-phone aerials, such as this one in Rome, will not be placed in residential areas.*

Rubbish and Recycling

Bottle banks, and bins for recycling plastic, aluminum, and biodegradable waste, are a common sight throughout Italy. However, in recycling, as in many other aspects of modern life, the south lags a long way behind the north. In 1998, 2.75 million tons of waste separated for recycling was collected in the north. In the center of the country this figure was about 500,440 tons, while in the south only 152,116 tons of separated trash was collected.

Land can also be "recycled." City councils often take old, disused land and turn it into areas that can be used by the community. This can include converting it into parks or playgrounds for the young, or even plots of land suitable for gardening, where people can enjoy growing their own fruit and vegetables.

▶ *These recycling bins have been painted and decorated by children in Pisa.*

IN THEIR OWN WORDS

"My name is Gianni. I work as a financial consultant. I recycle lots of things—paper, glass, plastics, and food waste. The council in my town has introduced all sorts of waste disposal bins and they're everywhere. I think it's very important to show that we do care about the environment—there are lots of things that we can't alter but we can help by recycling our trash. Even my mother, who is quite old, is very good at recycling—but I take the garbage out for her! We also have council dumps, where we can take the bulky things like old bikes and stoves."

6 The Changing Population

Birth rates and death rates in Italy are very similar (in 1999 there were 523,000 births and 566,000 deaths), so the overall population is fairly stable. People are generally living longer, fewer people are marrying, and fewer children are being born.

The birth rate and average family size tend to be higher in the south, where most rural people still have large families. Even so, there are some southern areas, such as Molise, Basilicata, and Calabria, where the population is falling as people move away in search of work.

An Aging Population

The life expectancy of Italians has risen rapidly over the past few decades. In 1961, the average man was living to 67, and the average woman was living to 72. By 1999, this had risen to 76 for men and 82 for women. There are many reasons for this longer lifespan, including a better standard of living, good healthcare, and a greater awareness of the importance of exercise and nutrition.

These days, the majority of Italians are between 20 and 69 years old, there are fewer children under 10, and more people over 75 years of age (particularly women) than in the past. Caring for this growing older generation is difficult. In the past, when extended families usually lived near one another, younger people could look after their older relatives. Now, with family members often living in different parts of the country, and an increasing number of women working, this has changed. Residential homes for the elderly are becoming more common, but unfortunately many old people often end up living on their own.

Population (millions)

100
90
80
70
60 — 57.3
50 — 47.1 · 53.8 · 54.4 (est.) · 41.2 (est.)
40
30
20
10
0
1950 1970 2000 2015 2050

Sources: 2000 and 2050 from United Nations Population Division; 1950 and 1970 from Geographical Digest; 2015 from United Nations Population Division.

▲ *The population of Italy has risen steadily since 1950, but is expected to fall by 2015.*

► *There are an increasing number of Italians who are over 75 years old.*

IN THEIR OWN WORDS

"My name is Melania and I am 17. Here I am with my sister Francesca. I'm on the left. I come from Sicily. Although Sicily is a part of Italy, Sicilians have a very strong regional identity. Three years ago, my family moved to Ravenna because my father found work here. At the beginning it was very difficult because all my friends were in Sicily, but now I like living here. I don't even want to go back to Sicily at Christmas—my life is here. For my mother, the most important thing was that our family stayed together. My sister Francesca is 32 and, now that she has found a job here, she is also quite settled. Sometimes I still feel 'Sicilian,' but most of the time I just feel Italian. This is my country, so I don't think it really matters where I live."

National Migration

Most of Italy's large, industrial, urban centers are in the north of the country. These towns and cities attract young people from the poorer areas with the promise of work. In particular, many people from the Alps, Apennines, Sicily, and Calabria have moved to the wealthier northern cities of Milan, Turin, and Genoa.

▶ *Three generations of this family live close together in the town of Porto Garibaldi in Ferrara. Although this was common in the past, the increase in national migration means that today, different members of the same family often live all over Italy.*

International Migration

In the early 20th century, a great many Italians migrated to the United States, South America, and Australia. Later, after World War II, the trend was for emigration to other European countries, particularly Germany, France, and Great Britain. Today, Italians are still emigrating, but in much smaller numbers. In the past, they left the country because they could not find work in Italy. Now they leave to find different work opportunities or lifestyles.

Meanwhile, more immigrants from other countries have decided to make Italy their home. In 2000, there were 1,270,553 foreign residents, a 13.8 percent increase over the previous year.

In 1986, the Italian government started trying to control immigration. Later, in the 1990s, Italy saw a huge increase in the number of immigrants from former Communist countries in Eastern Europe. Many of these people claimed to be refugees, and argued that their lives would be at risk if they were sent back to their own countries. Nowadays, illegal immigrants still try to enter Italy, particularly along the Adriatic coastline. If they do manage to get in undetected, it is very difficult to identify them and send them back to their country of origin.

▼ *People from all over the world migrate to Italy, where many make an important contribution to the workforce.*

Different parts of Italy tend to attract different groups of immigrants. For example, Sicily has a high number of North Africans, while along the Adriatic coast there are a lot of Albanians from the former Yugoslavia. Chinese and Philippine immigrants usually migrate toward the large centers, such as Milan, Turin, and Rome.

▶ *This fruit-packing factory employs women from all over the world—from Africa, Eastern Europe, and even South America.*

IN THEIR OWN WORDS

"My name is Jimena and I am 16. My family is part Italian and part Argentine. My father's parents went to Argentina before he was born. He grew up in Argentina and married my mother, and both my sister and I were born there. When I was five, the family moved back to Italy. Although I think of myself as Argentine, sometimes I feel more Italian. Where I live there is quite a big Argentine community, so my mother can see her friends and speak Spanish. We speak Spanish at home too. I think it is hardest for my mother. She misses her family in Argentina, but it costs so much to fly there that she can't go back very often."

Changes at Home

The Family

Italy has always been famous for its large families. Until about fifty years ago, particularly in the south of the country, it was not unusual to find families with as many as nine children. But today it is a very different story. There has been a rapid decline in the number of children per family. The average couple has only 1.2 children, compared to 2.67 in 1965. Italians are also deciding to have children later. In 1990, the average woman was 26 when she had her first child—now the average age is 28. Today, many people only choose to have children once they have found a good job, and the average young Italian, particularly in the wealthy northern areas of the country, tends to find permanent employment later than his or her parents. People who go to university graduate when they are about 24 or 25, and they may not find a stable job until they are about 27 years old.

IN THEIR OWN WORDS

"My name is Alessandro and I live with my partner Milena. We bought our own apartment two years ago, but we're not married yet. I don't think we'll marry until we decide to have children. We both have good jobs and we have a high standard of living. We can afford to go out with our friends a lot and we usually go on vacation abroad every year. Last year we went to Mexico, which was fantastic. Of course when we have children it will be different—so we want to enjoy ourselves now! We will probably only have one child and I think we will wait until my parents retire, so they can help us look after the baby."

◀ *In families where both parents work full-time, a baby-sitter is often employed to look after the children. This baby-sitter has her own children with her, as well as those she looks after.*

Many Italian women now choose to work, not merely for the extra income but also for the satisfaction and independence it gives them. In the past, if a mother chose to go out to work, there were always plenty of family members living close by who would look after the children. Now that many couples live away from their families, this is not possible. However, the government provides good childcare, with almost 95 percent of children between 3 and 6 years old attending nursery school.

▼ *This couple has just been married at a registry office. Many couples now choose not to marry in a church.*

Fewer people choose to marry than in the past. Many of those who do marry have a civil ceremony in a registry office, rather than a religious one in a church. (In 1999, civil marriages accounted for 23 percent of all marriages, compared to 1.6 percent in 1961.) Divorce and separation are more frequent; 37,224 separations were granted in 1988 and 62,737 in 1998.

Leisure

Sports are very important to Italians. Soccer is especially popular, and the majority of Italians follow the national league. Most young people play some sort of sport on a regular basis and take it very seriously. From the age of 6, when children start school, most of them participate in activities such as swimming, dancing, or playing an instrument.

In the summer, the beaches of the Adriatic are full of young people playing beach tennis and volleyball, and it is not unusual to find people in their 50s playing too. (Cycling is another favorite sport for those over 50.)

▲ *These young men are enjoying a game of soccer at Casal Borsetti, on the Adriatic coast.*

IN THEIR OWN WORDS

"My name is Mattias and I am 14. I used to play soccer when I was younger but now I play rugby. My mom is Scottish so she is very pleased— except when Scotland plays against Italy and then we don't know who to root for! I'm really glad that Italy has become a member of the Six Nations Rugby Tournament. Maybe now more people will start playing. Here, most people just think about soccer. I like playing rugby and this summer I'm going to two rugby camps in the north of Italy—I can't wait! My sisters go dancing a lot, so my mom is always busy either taking me to matches or taking my sisters to dancing school. She doesn't have much free time."

Less traditional sports—such as rugby, fencing, and various keep-fit activities—are becoming more popular; a regular visit to the gym is an important part of the Italian lifestyle, particularly for the 15-to-45 age group.

Young people also spend a lot of their free time using the latest technology. The majority of homes now have a personal computer and many young people like to spend their leisure time surfing the web, designing web pages, and socializing via e-mail.

◀ *Cycling is a very popular sport throughout Italy.*

Changes in Education

The Italian education system is split into three stages: ages 6–11 attend the *scuola elementare* (elementary school), 12–14 the *scuola media* (middle school), and 15–19 the *scuola superiore* (high school). When children leave the *scuola media*, they must choose a high school that specializes in science and technology, arts, classics, fine arts, or teaching. However, they still learn all the traditional subjects as well.

▲ *These children are on a school trip in Venice. School excursions may be to local places, to other areas in Italy, or, for high-school students, to a foreign country.*

Languages, computer skills, and other less traditional subjects are usually taught in schools nowadays. (From the age of 8 onward, children must learn a foreign language—usually English.) The average Italian school graduate has an incredible amount of knowledge, but limited experience in putting that knowledge to any practical use.

IN THEIR OWN WORDS

"My name is Paola, I am 16 and I go to high school. We study Latin, Greek, philosophy, and, of course, all the usual subjects such as math and Italian. We study English at school, but we don't do many hours so I also go to a private language school twice a week. I found it quite difficult to choose which high school to go to. I enjoy school, but it is hard work and we have to study a lot. I have about three hours of homework every day—too much!"

For this reason, schools are now being encouraged to become more practical and less theoretical.

There have been a great many changes in the Italian school system over the past few years. For example, in 1999 the government raised the compulsory school age from 14 to 15. Also, in the past, if students did not do well throughout the year, they could try to catch up over the summer. Now, they have to take another test at the beginning of the next school year and may even have to repeat the previous year. There has been talk of changing the system to two school stages rather than three, but no decision has been made.

Universities are mainly government funded and students pay annual taxes based on the family's income. About 30 percent of high school students go on to study at a university. It usually takes between four and six years to get a degree, depending on the subject.

◄ *Students outside their university in Pisa. Even after students graduate from university, many still have to take state exams for their chosen profession.*

Changes in Health

The state-funded *Servizio Sanitario Nazionale* (National Health Service) was introduced in Italy in 1978. This aims to offer an equal standard of care all over the country. Unfortunately, it does not always succeed. Some Italians in the south do not trust the public hospitals there—they are often old, badly maintained, and short-staffed. Several of these hospitals have been provided with new medical technology but they have few personnel qualified to operate it. As a result, a number of patients from the south go to private health clinics or travel to the north, where hospitals are more efficient and better staffed.

Prescription charges for medicines (called "tickets") were introduced in the mid-1990s, for everyone except the terminally ill, people on a low income, pensioners, and children under 6. The state also provides dental treatment, but the majority of Italians choose to pay a dentist privately.

Italians are very concerned about their health system, which is expensive to run and sometimes inefficient. In the future, there will certainly be further changes, such as giving patients a wider choice of treatments, and maybe even including some forms of alternative medicine. Homeopathy, naturopathy, and other types of alternative medicine are available to Italians if they are willing to pay, but it will be some time before these treatments are offered through the National Health Service.

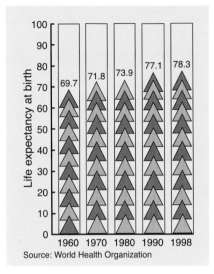

▲ *The improved Italian health service is one reason for the rise in life expectancy of Italians.*

▶ *An ambulance waits outside the ambulance station in Pisa. The Italian health service has improved greatly over the past twenty-five years, but still faces many challenges.*

Changing Diet

The traditional Italian diet (pasta, meat, fish, and salad with plenty of olive oil) is very healthy. But today, life moves at a faster pace, and there is no longer as much time to sit down and enjoy food as in the past. Fast-food restaurants (serving burgers and fries) are becoming popular. These restaurants use advertising to target children, in the hope of changing people's ideas about food and eating, early in life. At present, Italians still eat home-cooked food more than ready-made, pre-packed meals from supermarkets. However, with more women going out to work, and people having fewer children later in life, this is also changing.

▲ *Fruit and vegetables form a major part of the traditional Italian diet.*

► *A fast-food restaurant. Fast food is becoming an increasingly popular option for young people and busy families.*

IN THEIR OWN WORDS

"My name is Claudio and I am a pensioner. I spend a lot of my time on my land growing vegetables for my wife and my daughters. My wife is a very good cook—but my daughters are a bit lazy in the kitchen—they never seem to have time to cook! On Sundays, my two daughters come to our house with their families and we all sit down to a big family meal—my wife even makes fresh pasta on Sundays and on special holidays like Christmas or Easter. I think it's sad that young families are too busy to sit down and enjoy their meals all together—my grandchildren just want to eat in fast-food restaurants!"

Religion

Catholicism became the official religion of Italy in 1929. In 1984, an agreement between the Italian state and the Catholic Church reduced the Church's influence over Italian society. Religious education at school is no longer compulsory and state funding of the Church has been substantially reduced.

Today, 90 percent of Italians are Catholic, but the number of practicing Catholics is falling. Almost all children still go through the rituals of First Communion and Confirmation, taking special lessons one day a week—for three years for their First Communion, and for another two years for Confirmation. For many, this is more a case of following tradition than religious devotion.

The Catholic Church, under the leadership of the Pope, has always been strongly opposed to divorce and abortion. But in the 1970s, Italians voted to legalize divorce and abortion. This is an example of how, over recent decades, the Italians have changed their views on religion. Although they consider themselves Catholic, most do not apply all the teachings of Catholicism to their daily lives.

▲ *People attending church on a Sunday morning. Over the past fifty years, the number of Italians who go to church regularly has fallen dramatically.*

IN THEIR OWN WORDS

"My name is Don Paolo and I am a priest. I'm 33—much younger than most of the priests you see in Italy. It's sad that not many people go into the Church any more. It's good being a young priest, because I can talk to young people more easily than some of my older colleagues. Unfortunately, some of the older people in my parish seem to think of me as a child. A lot of young people come to our church to meet their friends—it's a bit like a youth club. Unfortunately, not many of them actually go to church services—but I'm still pleased that they come here to socialize."

There are 225,000 Protestants in Italy. And, as more immigrant workers come into the country, there are increasing numbers of non-Christians (particularly Muslims). The majority of Italian Jews were killed in Nazi concentration camps during World War II, but many Jews have migrated to Italy since then. In 1987, the Jewish community gained the right not to work on Saturday (the Jewish Sabbath)—an indication of the increasing respect Italians have for different religious beliefs.

▼ *These nuns are shopping at a street market. Despite the change in the number of practicing Catholics, many nursery and primary schools in Italy are still run by nuns.*

8 Changes at Work

Manufacturing

After World War II, with the help of the European Recovery Fund (or Marshall Plan), the European Coal and Steel Community (ECSC), and the European Economic Community (EEC), Italy was able to develop its steel production rapidly. By 1980, the country was producing 21 percent of European steel (only West Germany produced more). The steel industry was one of the most productive Italian industries in the post-war period, but it has since suffered from strong competition from Japanese steel manufacturers. Gradually, the supply of steel has exceeded demand, and it has become harder for Italian manufacturers to sell the steel they produce.

The motor industry in the north of the country (Fiat in Turin, Alfa Romeo and Lancia in Milan) was very successful until the 1980s, but, once again, competition from Japan meant that production in Italy decreased.

▼ *Although the motor industry in Italy is lowering its output, Italian-made motorbikes and cars, such as this MV Augusta F4, are still considered to be among the best in the world.*

In contrast, the chemical and pharmaceutical industries, and the fertilizer, petrochemical, and synthetic rubber and resin manufacturers, are doing very well. However, because the chemical industry has to import so many raw materials, it is very sensitive to international factors such as the price of oil. The chemical industry also has to face the problem of increased safety and environmental regulations, imposed by the Italian state and the EEC. These regulations are certainly important, but they make the industry less competitive on the world market. For example, because an Italian company has to follow all these regulations, it takes much longer to open a new plant than it would in most other countries.

▲ *Many industries in Italy have to conform to tough anti-pollution regulations. This power station is only a mile or two from the busy beaches of the northern Adriatic coast and must ensure that it meets strict environmental laws.*

IN THEIR OWN WORDS

"My name is Anna-Maria and I am the Health, Safety, and Environmental Officer for a chemical plant in the north of Italy. I like my job, but these days it is very difficult. I have to keep up to date with all the new laws and regulations—and there are so many! I seem to spend all my time reading. Italians worry much more now about safety at work, and even more about the environment, than they did in the past. I think this is a good thing. The chemical industry is very important for so many aspects of our everyday life, but we must respect the environment at the same time. My company even has extra environmental certificates that are not required by law, because it takes environmental matters so seriously."

The New Working Environment

In 1960, 25 percent of the working population was employed in agriculture. In 1995, this had fallen to less than 8 percent. Medium-sized farms (those between 15 and 250 acres) take up almost half of all arable land in Italy. But the owners of these farms are increasingly leaving the land for the town, in order to take up better-paid employment.

Service industries now employ well over 50 percent of the working population and account for almost 60 percent of Italy's gross national product (GNP). This service sector includes tourism, public services, transportation, finance, and information technology. The traditional factory worker or farm laborer has been replaced by the highly computer-literate office worker. Office work is generally better-paid than factory or farm work, and the standard of living of many Italians has therefore risen. However, these changes also mean that many manufacturing industries now have difficulty finding manual laborers.

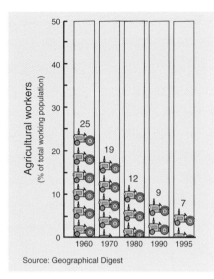

Source: Geographical Digest

▲ *This graph shows the dramatic drop in the number of Italians working in agriculture.*

▼ *Internet cafés such as this one have recently become big businesses in major cities for tourists and residents alike.*

A number of people now work from home, using information technology to keep in touch with their workplace. Others are choosing to be self-employed, rather than compete for a permanent position in a company. Self-employment, whether freelance or on short-term contracts, is an increasingly popular option.

Women at Work

The role of women within the labor market has also changed. In theory, women should receive equal pay and status. However, while women hold many important positions, and have moved into what were once considered male-dominated fields (as magistrates, journalists, politicians, and engineers, for example), it is still difficult for them to rise to senior management positions. Some women claim this is a result of discrimination. Despite generous maternity-leave arrangements, some believe that the state does not provide enough help to enable employees to combine running a home with furthering a career. As women usually take more responsibility for the home and children than their husbands, this means that they are more likely to be disadvantaged at work.

▲ *Like many other women today, this warehouse worker is doing a job that a few years ago would have been considered suitable only for a man.*

IN THEIR OWN WORDS

"My name is Maria and I'm a Quality Control Officer for an industrial plant. It is a wonderful job but, now that I have twin daughters, I find it difficult to fit everything in. Before my children were born, I used to stay in the office until after 8 o'clock every night, but now I try to leave earlier. Luckily, I can work a sort of flexi-time, so in the morning I don't come into the office until 9:30. This means that I can take my children to school. My parents-in-law live near us, so if the children are ill or on vacation from school they can stay with them. Life is hectic, but I love my job and I love being a mother."

The Way Ahead

Italy has come a long way since World War II. It is a member of G8 (the eight richest industrial countries in the world), after the United States, Japan, Germany, and France but ahead of Great Britain. There are several reasons for its rapid progress over the last fifty years. First, international assistance immediately after the war helped Italy's economy to grow. Secondly, government policy over the years has stabilized the country politically and economically. And thirdly, hard work by the Italians has ensured that the economy has continued to grow. The word *sacrifici* is very important in Italy—it means you never achieve anything without making sacrifices. Perhaps this idea has helped the country become stronger.

◀ *Italy is now a full member of the European Community. Here the Italian flag and the flag of the European Economic Community fly side by side.*

IN THEIR OWN WORDS

"My name is Giulia and I'm 17. Next year I will finish school and go to university. I feel optimistic about my future and the future of my country. I know that there will be difficult times for me on a personal level. Will I find a job? Will I be able to stay near my family? If I think about the future of Italy the first thing I think of is the euro—it is strange without the lira but I think it is a positive step. I hope it will help make the world a "smaller" place. The only big worry I have for the future is about the environment and global warming. I realize that today people know the risks and in general they are trying to improve the situation. I just hope that it is not too late—but I am optimistic about that too."

Many Italians still want to see more changes. Unfortunately, the division between north and south is as deep today as it was at the end of the war. In order to keep the support of the wealthier north, the government has to find a way of developing the south without damaging the rest of the country financially. If this issue can be resolved, then the country as a whole may finally be united politically, economically, and culturally.

The other critical questions that Italians are concerned about are those of immigration, crime, education, and health. These are areas that affect everyone and in recent years the government has done much to improve the situation—regulating immigration into Italy, introducing tougher laws on crime, and reforming the educational and health systems.

While there is still much to be done, the achievements of the past few decades mean that Italians can be confident about their country's future.

▼ *Italy's rich cultural heritage continues to be important today. This is part of the set for a modern production of the Italian opera* La Traviata, *being wheeled toward the Roman arena in Verona.*

Glossary

Agriculture The use of land to produce crops for food or other purposes.

Biodegradable Able to decompose naturally.

Birth rate The number of people born in a particular place over a given period of time.

Economy All the business activity in a country.

Electromagnetic smog Pollution caused by radiation from aerials and pylons.

Emigration People leaving their country of nationality to move to another country to live permanently.

Export Selling goods or services to foreign countries.

Fascist A system in which the government has great control over most aspects of citizens' lives. A fascist government is often controlled by the army.

GNP GNP stands for Gross National Product, the total amount of money earned by all a country's businesses in a year. 'Per capita' is Latin and means 'per person'. GNP per capita is the figure you reach by dividing the total wealth produced by the total population.

Grants Money given by the government to particular groups or organizations for specific reasons.

Hydroelectric power Using the force of falling water to generate electricity.

Immigration People coming into one country from another to live permanently.

Import Buying goods from foreign countries.

Lagoon A shallow lake.

Landslides The movement of large amounts of land, usually after very heavy rain.

Life expectancy How long people are expected to live.

Livestock Animals that are kept on a farm.

Media Newspapers, television and radio.

Migration When people move to other areas within a country.

Mineral A hard substance, such as coal, that is dug out of the ground.

Municipalities Similar to councils, these are the most local form of government. The municipalities are responsible for the day to day running of the cities.

Nun A member of a religious community of women.

Nuclear power Electricity made from the energy of splitting atoms.

Organic Produce Fruit and vegetables produced without the use of fertilizers and pesticides.

Population The total number of people in a particular area such as a town or country.

Refugees People who leave their homeland because of war, poverty or political unrest.

Registry office A government office where legal ceremonies, such as weddings, can be performed.

Right-wing The conservative section of a population or party.

Rural In the country.

Subsidence When land begins to sink below its original level.

Urban In the city.

Further Information

Books

Arnold, Helen. *Postcards from Italy (Postcards From)*. New York: Raintree Steck-Vaughn Publishing, 2000.

Blashfield, Jean F. *Enchantment of the World, Second Series: Italy*. Danbury, CT: Children's Press, 1999.

Frank, Nicole. *Welcome to My Country: Welcome to Italy*. Milwaukee, WI: Gareth Stevens, Inc., 2000.

Harvey, Miles. *Metropolis: Look What Came from Italy*. Danbury, CT: Franklin Watts, Inc., 1999.

Martin, Fred. *Next Stop Italy*. Chicago, IL: Heinemann Library, 1998.

Nickles, Greg. *Lands, People, and Cultures: Italy—the Land*. New York: Crabtree Publishing, 2001.

Petersen, Christine. *True Book: Italy*. Danbury, CT: Children's Press, 2001.

Ross, Stewart. *Fact or Faction: Conquerors and Explorers*. Brookfield, CT: Copper Breech Books, 1996.

Useful addresses

Embassy of Italy in the United States
3000 Whitehaven Street, N.W.
Washington, D.C. 20008

UNICO National, Inc.
Fairfield Commons
271 US Highway 46 West
Suite A-108
Fairfield, New Jersey 07004

Websites

www.odci.gov/cia/publications/factbook
Information about Italy from the CIA Factbook, including material on Italian geography, population, economy and politics.

www.realitaly.com
A site promoting the cultural, artistic and natural heritage of Italy. Contains information about monuments, museums and the history of Italy.

www.italytour.com
This site offers a virtual tour of Italy, and includes information about Italian news and media, and arts and culture.

www.cultureitaly.com
An online magazine selling Italian products, but also including extensive information about the history and culture of Italy.

Index

Page numbers in **bold** refer to photographs, maps or statistics panels.

Adriatic, the **5**, 8, 10, 11, 14, **21**, 28, 29, 32, **32**, 41
agriculture 9, 12, 18–19, **18**, **19**, 42
  organic 18, 19

beaches 10, 11, **11**, 23, 32

Capri 10
climate 9, 11, 12–13, **12**, 18
coasts 10–11, 13, 14, 16, 32
  erosion of 11, 14
Communist Party 6, **6**
crime 45
currency 5, 45

earthquakes 10
economy 6, 7, 44, 45
education 7, 31, 34–35, **34**, **35**, 38, **39**, 45
Elba **5**, 14
emigration 28
energy sources 15
environment 8, 22, 23, 41, 45
environmental groups 14, 22, 23
European Coal and Steel Community (ECSC) 6, 7, 40
European Economic Community (EEC) 7, 11, 40, 41, **44**
European Recovery Fund 6, 40
European Union 23
exports 18, 19

family life 26, 27, **27**, 30–31, **31**, 37
fishing 16, **16**, 17, **17**
flag **44**
floods 13, **13**
food **16**, 37, **37**

Genoa 4, 5, **5**, 9, 13, 27
government 6, 7, 8, 13, 21, 22, 23, 24, 28, 35, 44, 45

Grand Canal **13**
Gross National Product (GNP) **7**, 42

health 26, 36, **36**, 37, 41, 45
housing 20–21, **20**

immigrants 28–29, **28–29**, 39, 45
imports 7, 14, 15, 16
industry 4, 7, 14, 15, 16, 17, **17**, 23, **23**, 27, 40–41, **40**, **41**, 42, 43
information technology 4, 33, 34, 42, **42**, 43
irrigation **19**

lakes
  Como 5, 9
  Garda 5, 9, **9**
  Maggiore 5, 9
landscape 8–11, 21
landslides 21
languages 5, 29, 34
leisure 11, 32–33, **32**, **33**
life expectancy 26

Marshall Plan (*see European Recovery Fund*)
Milan 4, **4**, 5, **5**, 12, **20**, 27, 40
mountains 5, 8, 9, **9**, 10
  Alps 9, **9**, 15, 27
  Apennines 9, 27
  Dolomites 9
  Monte Bianco (Mont Blanc) 5, 9
Mussolini, Benito 6

Naples 5, **5**, 10
natural resources 14–19

Palermo 5, **5**
parks 8
Pisa 5, **6**, **11**, **25**, **35**, **36**
politics 6, 7, 13, 44, 45
pollution 11, 13, 16, 20, 22, **22**, 23, **23**, 24, 41

population 5, 26
  density 5
  growth 20
  rural 7, 20
power stations 15, **41**

recycling 23, 24, 25, **25**
religion 5, 31, 38–39, **38**, **39**
rivers 5, 8, 11, 23
  Adige **5**, 8
  Po **5**, 8, 15
  Tiber **5**, 8
Roman Empire 6
Rome 5, **5**, 6, 7, 8, 20, 29

Sardinia 10, 13, 14, 18
shopping 4, **4**, **16**, 39
Sicily **5**, 10, 15, 16, 27, 29
sport 32, **32**, 33, **33**

tourism 4, 11, 23, 42, **42**
transport 4, **4**, 20, 22, **22**, 40, **40**, 42
Turin 4, 5, **5**, 27, 29, 40
Tuscany **5**, **11**, 14

urban expansion 20, 27, 42

Venice 5, 8, 13, **13**
Verona 5, 20, **45**
volcanoes
  Etna 10, **10**
  Vesuvius 10

water 15, 23
  power 15
  supply **15**
wildlife 8
World War II 6, 28, 39, 40, 44, 45